Physics for Beginners

JOHN PETER HARN

BLUE LIGHT PRESS ◆ 1ST WORLD PUBLISHING

SAN FRANCISCO ◆ FAIRFIELD ◆ DELHI

WINNER OF THE **2017** BLUE LIGHT BOOK AWARD

PHYSICS FOR BEGINNERS

Copyright ©2018 by John Peter Harn

1ST WORLD LIBRARY
PO Box 2211
Fairfield, IA 52556
www.1stworldpublishing.com

BLUE LIGHT PRESS
www.bluelightpress.com
Email: bluelightpress@aol.com

BOOK & COVER DESIGN
Melanie Gendron
melaniegendron999@gmail.com

FRONT COVER ART
Deborah Bracken Michel

AUTHOR PHOTO
Etsuko Matsunaga Harn

FIRST EDITION

Library of Congress Control Number: 2017953706

ISBN 9781421837833

*This book is dedicated to anyone
who wants to know who their real mother was
and which of the billion minor gods
we call stars
kept her up all night dancing.*

In memory of Daniel Thomas Harn, 1952–2017

Contents

To Soften the End

In Asia Minor

a slave girl's beauty flared
one summer and burned a few years
but only her wash basin knew it.

In the back of a shop
on the main street in Ephesus
she pounded leather
knew the kindling
knew the bellows.

An olive voice. A chiseled face.
Dark eyes in a sea of ivory.

She had one memory
of the time before.
Everyone singing at the end of a life.
Roasted lamb on her mother's breath.

This Ecstasy Because

I became you
once in a lost slice of time.
Became your fingerprints
the unzipped DNA in your eyes
the star map your history
sleeps rolled up in.
And in return for that
mother lode I fell
into a well, illuminated
on the way down by a blue-green opium haze
the scar of which I'll keep
as long as I have skin.

They say Medieval nuns
broken by work and bound by celibacy
touched ecstasy
in the light the soul
of Christ gave off.

Inside in a listless prayer. Cloistered.
Apple blossoms blown upslope.

Everything You Took

you'll give back.
You'll find yourself
in a dormant garden
gone to seed
puffing frozen air.

Your version might be
to dig up stones you played with as a child
and wedge them in the powdered roots
of a tree returned to smoke.

Or maybe you'll slip twigs under the floorboards
of your ancestor's weatherboarded cabin
next to the desiccated corn
and skeletal leaves already there.

Like everyone else
you'll find a way
to nudge a translucent apple
with a transparent toe.

All of it:
Parched bits of script.
A campfire shadow on a cliff face.
A hairbrush in a tattered velvet box.
Everything you thought you had.

Jewelry On

Loner child, I grew vegetables
for the family table
in a patch outside the garage.
Standing in the doorway
gnarled carrots in my hands
I realized the ancient soil
was full of bone.

The past is a number
at the end of a fingertip
dialed back to zero.
It's a telephone
not ringing in a carpeted hallway.
It's not the feather
but the feather falling.

In a hospice room
deep inside her favorite perfume
an old woman cradles
her smiling face in her papery hands.
Every ring and bracelet on
she laughs and laughs and laughs.

On a Thailand Beach

alone in a hammock strung between palms
my heartbeat's aligned
with waves' punctual foam in moonlight.

I'll lie here all night if I have to
and I have to
dozing in and out of life
until dawn arrives
and I push my wasted skeleton
along the beach to search for shells
where I'll pinch a few
delicate defective ones
carry them home to a different ocean
ending a different continent
and at an astronomically precise
random moment
drop them in that other surf.

It's the least adorned ritual
hovering in the neutral zone
between sentiment and revelation
I can think of by myself.

Saltwater. Seaweed. Drifted wood.
Eventually this beach will be like me
just another carbon scrawl
once legible at the bottom of a page.

Even alone I say too much.

Dreaming of Happiness

beats watching styrofoam
roll in and out with the tide.

Did we just tap a happiness vein, you and I?
Shape-shifting through the Yukon
in a vintage train's observation car?
Because my rebuilt bones think so.

First, you stopped me from cooking
corned beef and cabbage
because that's what the paisley
redesign of our aesthetic was for.
To make us not care
what we forgot to remember.

Then our conjoined pasts flew by
locked in a gangly octave.

Painting a fresco helped too.
And the laughter, antibiotic
exhumed from my gut by your backhoe antics
making us siblings on banana-seat bikes
exhausted in the shade of a grandfather oak.

So. A toast then. To you, my friend.
To our luck having wasted
some hours untethered together
fanning flames and wondering what if
we really were soaring
over mundane turf like high-wire sages.

Oregon in Fall

Brown reeds and cattails.
Cold new grass below the water line.
Weeks of rain in wetlands
between September's drought
and January's hard freeze.

Twenty-eight years ago a prisoner
at the Oregon State Pen
twenty-five years for murder
slipped me a folded poem he wrote
about looking up at geese
from the exercise yard
because their calls found him
and their 'V' pointed elsewhere.

I can't remember his eyes
or any real word in his poem.
But ever since, whatever useless thing
I'm doing in November
when geese puncture the impervious
dome above me, I look up
for as long as it takes to find them.

And I always find them.
Geese the poet and I
keeping faith in Oregon.

Postcard from Seattle

for Scott

So this is Pike Street Market
where Suquamish Indians invented prosperity
before work came along
and ruined everything.

Maybe one of these starving seagulls still carries
a chip of Suquamish bone
in a corner of its debris-pouch stomach.
Or maybe ribbons of their DNA still weave
through stubby midden piles
under these floorboards and pilings
waiting for a sixty-foot wave
to unwrite their eulogy.

Is there just enough dust of them left
on sidewalks and rooftops around here
to get sucked up in a cold front
crest the Cascades and fall out
like volcanic ash on your hometown?

And do you think we mixed some
into your garden that weekend
in the nineties when we drank bourbon
from coffee cups in your Salvation Army lawn chairs
trying to coax potatoes
from the soil to the stew
by buffoonery alone?

I remember feeling back then
we could have that weekend again
any time we wanted.
They felt that too, you know. Young Suquamish men
squandering their own back-lit youth
shirking, like us, responsibility.

Chief Seattle's speech
to Governor Stevens is for sale here
framed or rolled up
on parchment for tourists.
Like it or not I'm sending you one
as a reminder.
But of what you'll have to tell me.

Climbing Mt. Fuji at Night

With the first step I agreed to fall
into metaphor the second
dawn broke and torched the summit.

Slapstick partners, a volcano still hot
from unwrapping itself and me
a sarcastic clown from the city
braided in a way only the alpine grass understood.

Climbing all night on broken legs
giving up water faster than I could replace it
I made it somehow
to the crater's honeyed bowl
Roman nose parting the strong east wind
waiting for sunrise.

Climbing a volcano at night
is the most blatant metaphor.
Struggling for toeholds in the dark
risking it all just to teeter
on a sulfured lip at dawn
embracing poverty
waiting for illumination in the frozen dark.

I expected all that. Paid for it even.
But a no-show sun obscured by clouds?
That I got for free.

Gray Cemetery, Schuyler County Illinois

The irony of *It Came and Went*
carved into a headstone.
Benjamin Davis. Died
1837. 61 years.

Was it those four words
because a comet hung
in a corner of the night sky the week you died
a keyhole to the afterlife?

Or did a temporary spell
of perfect weather volunteer
to soften the end of your illness
letting you and your bereaved
linger in the sound of rustling leaves?

Or did you choose those words yourself
after green light leapt
from a log you split for the fire?

If a descendant touches your headstone
it won't matter if he knows
a thing about his buckshot ancestry.
Your stone will crumble in the next light rain.

Because the Economic Imperative

lies in the gap between him and his truck
a balding high school English teacher
endures another platitude.

After work, red wine and a rusty shot
of history. Old letters from a shoebox.
Postmarks worn as buffalo nickels.

Three AM, bare chested, stir-fry on the stove
he walks the wet streets alone
plucks an idea from the proprietary contrail
of his linear life.

Glassy but clean-shaven
he's on time for the first period bell.

Okay people, listen up.
Today we're going to have a debate
so we'll make two teams.
All of you who never asked to be born
raise your fucking hands…

Somewhere in America

a woman spoon feeds soup
to her husband of fifty years.
When he's done, she dabs his chin with a washcloth
kisses the top of his head
and takes his bowl to the sink.

The beetle-bored timbers that frame his memory
recall the contents of a lost box
but not the woman in front of him
the fulcrum and counterweight
at his table five decades
waiting in mist now
for the never quite arriving
tipping point to arrive.

She rinses out his bowl
ladles some soup for herself
and sits across from him to eat.

In the space between
a giant black oak and a shuttered white house
he plays with a small red dog.

How Many Things

do I really need to know?
The ins and outs of the doubled elastic soul
lovers own?
            Certainly.

And where to find the backlit maples
of my early years?
            That too.

And how to replay the speech
I made to my first girlfriend
underneath one of those backlit maples?
            Maybe not.

And whether I get to keep
the chip of my own fossil bone
found protruding from a riverbank
by children on a field trip?
            No. No. No.

And which of my ingrate descendants
will toss that bone out on moving day?
            (I'll settle for knowing
            where my wandering hands and feet are.)

Physics for Beginners

It's Tempting to Thank

the billion years of single-cells
for everything that came after.
For the first obsidian blade
and papyrus strong enough
to hoist a limestone ton.
For geometry
squatting over Pharaoh's bones
and the illiterate geniuses at Petra
chiseling all the rock
that wasn't a temple away.
For the wine-stained French
wrestling gravity to a draw
Franklin's key
and the bravehearts who forged
a Mars rover from a dab of magma.
Because without all of those
quenchless thirsts, each one built
from the bones of the others
your laugh wouldn't have pinged my parabolic heart.

A Poet's Guide to the Natural Sciences

1. The Big Bang

White draws a deep breath
and coughs up the spectrum
on a stainless-steel table
already scattered with diamonds.

There's agreement on three things.
It chewed through time with a tungsten bit.
It unbraided a billion-strand weave.
Life is tethered there.

To get the basic outline
examine the backs of your hands.
It'll end up true if you start with a circle.

2. Quantum Mechanics

Hard drugs are required
for proper assembly.
Make sure you have all the parts.
First, use the aptitude wrench
to loosen the rotating hexagons.
Then give up. This is a journey to the center.

A two-story billiard table
exists in seven dimensions
in your head.
Your cue passes through an iron ball.
A hologram of you applauds
in three, no, zero places.
Paint flakes assemble
the Mona Lisa on a black glass floor.

Particles, waves, a tongue of fire and you
gripping the four corners of uncertainty.

3. The Origin of Life

You're working in your father's garage
trying to find the source
of a knock in your daughter's car.
You travel the length of a hose
hand over hand, looking for a bulge
crimp, tear or fork, but
no. It's a straight shot back
to the engine block itself
where life began
where your garage began
on the tensile surface of a moment exploded.

If you need proof
look in the preamble to the periodic chart.
It's hanging on the pegboard
where the girls of Honolulu
calendar used to be.

4. Photosynthesis

They grew up fast, the chosen ones.
They who found the liquor cabinet
locked and snapped the chain.

No more ankle-deep in grey water.
No more table scraps.

Authors of genius in a righteous fury
they incorporated a star
and so became
deities apart.

5. Evolution

No one will offer
to scrape the molasses barrel with you.
So you'll have to like molasses.

Darwin didn't tell the whole story.
For example how life
evolved itself on purpose.

Keep it away from wooden stakes and open flame.
Use in areas with well-marked exits.
It has no effect on people with immune systems.

Parents, start with the basics.
Walk your children into a room
the exact moment other people leave.
Make sure your children notice the substitution.
It doesn't take a genius.

6. Mass Extinctions

Don't be too impressed
holding title to your land.
You are caretaking a saturated soil.

Wildly disturbing things have happened.
We carry the muscle memory
bone crystals, echoes in our ears.

The first time was nothing much.
A scaffolding of sea foam was hit by a wave.
Recombinants and opportunists swarmed in
sorted things out.

Eventually, ants will be in charge.
Hunger knows how to restring the bow.

7. The Size of the Universe

Try out a scale model or two for perspective.
Divide the calendar year
into thousandths of a second.
Or score a fifty-mile straightaway
with reflective white paint.
Have some fun.
But it won't help.

The Greeks knew about the great beyond.
That all lines were curved.
That smallest and largest consumed each other's tails.

Oh to have seen them with their eyes on fire
stained in red wine and firelight
panning the elements from a rocky stream.

Under the Milky Way, after midnight
Democritus asked Leucippus
If we peered over the farthest edge
would we see the backs of our heads?

Drunk bastards.
They knew how to get around.

8. Extraterrestrials

The short answer is no
and the long is of course.

But not the bug-eyed kind with a suction-cup nose.
Rather, a puree.
A half tissue, half excrement
sky's-the-limit ambitious ooze
in our own back yard, on Mars
or a shave-ice moon.

But if it's not close by
and if we have to go long . . .
we'll need to kiss our photons goodbye.

Hello jubilee, hello extinction.
We come in peace.

Unity

Mt. Blanc's glacier equals
Patagonia's bedrock.
A brass doorknob equals
an unwashed monk.
A slug trail on the cover
of your hymnal in moonlight.
A Kikuyu banana grove
in a Gettysburg downpour.
A therapist at Stonehenge.
Your fifth-grade love.
A Triceratops femur.
A Nez Perce sweat lodge.
White mums on a casket.
Arctic core samples.
Lindbergh's memoir.
Canadian heather.
Buffalo nickels.
Clay.

The core of the sun equals
your freckled shoulders.
What has always equals
what has never really been.

Once We Bred with the Gods

right on the surface of the earth.
In fact,

we were the gods
and we were the surface of the earth.

Firelight helped us
pull incantations from each other.
There weren't many of us
but we were waterproof
drinking from the zodiac
chasing grass.

We left almost nothing behind
footprints and postholes
a bone flute in the ashes.

6 AM and I'm driving to work
hands on the wheel
inside the lines.

Tree Bark

for Mark Matisoff 1960-2012

How little it takes to end something
so long in the making.
A word. A barrel flash.
The underside of a boot
finding chemistry's miracle
on a sidewalk.

What isn't you becomes you
for a time, immeasurable
then moves on. Tree bark
already humus
becomes spider silk
a polymer
a reactive gas reacting.

Even these words
are already this page's curly ash
while the eyes that might have read them
ride a pollen wave dispersed.

Walk Forever

if you have to.

See if the moon over Asia
is the same moon.
Step from a forest
into a city or vice versa.

Use books for shoes
bark for money.
Doze in the intimate generosity
of dappled shade
or wait for a bus
in the slender shadow of a power pole.

Keep an eye on the pigeons
dotting the doric bank's car-honk roofline.
Or let yourself be hypnotized
by stones in a tannin stream.

Carve new hands from new wood.
Decide if the season's first snow
unleashing silence
will erase or just hide you.

Success is an Ibex

butchered downwind of the big cats.
Young lovers, engaged for months
cross a busy intersection
their interlaced hands
filter nutrients from city air.

At a shopping mall, holding something sheer
against herself in a dressing room
she unzips the double helix
as an eagle's cry pierces
muzak's waterfall.

He waits for her on an ottoman
between stores.
Tapping his cell phone
napped flint at his feet.

If he meets his sales goal
she'll produce an extra ounce of milk.
If she enrolls in night school
he'll find a fig tree
ripening in the parking lot.

Salmon taste fresh water.
Elk won't graze a valley cul-de-sac.
A digging stick intuits roots.

What Exactly

for Chako

is a lifeless body
beautiful on the kitchen floor.

Is it more than flesh
engineered by rotations
of a celestial take-your-pick
invulnerable at last and mixing with air?

When does the dispersed negation
of the big bang
suspended either side of living
let us back in.

Let's say a hand strokes a lifeless body
with a trace of warmth left in it.

Does the hydrogen dream take one and not the other?

Backlit

by a floor-to-ceiling window
a young woman in a coffee shop
gathers her hair in both hands
to make a ponytail.

She's not old enough
to know how implausible that is
how any one thing could've stopped her
how many defeated outcomes
wait in the lie of empty space

like where she'll land and
whose name she'll call out.
Whether she'll be heard.

This Singularity

A diffuse light scrubs
silence from thin air
and exhales it into me
which means it's almost my turn.

Drab leaves amend a soil.
Bright leaves amend a soil.
The earth doesn't care what feeds it.

Everything We Know

will be sterilized and dumped
on another eon's doorstep.

No remnant of your singing voice.
No tremor from the hardest kiss you ever had.
None of the tracks you left
crawling over coals
piled up against your deathbed.

Nothing will survive this frozen earth
slamming into its resurrection
scattering the clutch of relic sea stars
in its Mother Theresa arms.

But we can say we had a kingdom once.

As If

Maybe It Should Go Unnoticed

this space between my face
and those birds raising havoc
in my neighbor's yard.

Maybe what's unexplainable
shouldn't be explained.
The light in a miner's eye.
The smell of revolution
on a factory floor.

Every day, random things are spelled backwards.
Only yesterday a diesel
hauled porcelain dolls
over a rutted mountain road
wiping out
a lost hiker's footprints.

Even this ink, you know
is just air.
Less, probably.

Daily Walk

A glass of water evaporates
in the kitchen of my tiny house.
Above the tight grey weave of January clouds
the sun stalls.
Not yet dusted in volcanic ash
I'll do anything
not to walk in ordinary light.

My neighbor says eternity sleeps
at the edge of a bean field.
I could walk there I guess
stroll through the place each of us was conceived
paddle through the remnants of the old ones' sighs.

But the earth has no contour lines
and my map, smeared from being
under water so long
lacks a compass rose.

Slanted rays now and a bold yellow light
so off I go on foot.
A wet finger tests the air.
From every direction, white.
Then a bagpipe.

Only a Dotted Line Connects

what could be
to what is

and whoever draws it undotted
may not have actually started
breathing at birth
learning instead to shadow-breathe
and stayed with that not knowing
there was another way.

For example:
A man rolls out of bed in the morning
and across his bedroom floor.
He rappels down stairs to the kitchen
and makes breakfast with his feet
tiptoeing over appliances
as if they were dabs of fragile beauty.

And then they are dabs of fragile beauty.

It Seemed to Him that No One

showed up for work at the call center
although everyone was there
on time waiting
for his morning pep-talk.
But just his gaze
washed over them this time
from a shaft of sunlight
no one could remember
the color of.
And when he unzipped
the skin-tight suit he'd poured
three decades of work into
and tiptoed out
mute and unencumbered
with the taste of lemon in his mouth
light poured from his eyes
as light poured from theirs
each now forever a part
of the other's illusion.

Passport

When did I become this
charcoal sphere in a head scarf.
This babushka rattling a padlocked gate.
An engraved brass plaque
is stuck to the palm of my hand.
I wave it at windows
but don't catch a thing.
I flash it at a taxi but the taxi blows away.
When a city bus grabs the curb
exploding air brakes
suck blood from my heart.
The driver knows I have gold.
He lets me join the other
charcoal spheres en route.
I rub it with my thumb
sounding out the foreign words.
Once I bought a potato with it
but it grew a knobby sprout.
Once I got inside the Grand Hotel with it
the doorman let me pass.
Curly mail boxes scaled a lobby wall
until a siren chased me out
and an alley spooned me back.
An engraved brass plaque
is stuck to the palm of my hand.
If I press my palms together
and pillow my head against the glass
I sleep like a swan.
It's quiet here, between day and night.
When it warms up, this bus is a fancy ship.
Windows steamed over
nobody knows we're here.

Advice

Believe me
whoever I am.
Don't be a person
who paints seagulls.
Because I have eyes
lead me down a primrose path.
Because I'm reflective
tell me things you don't know yet.
Be open
to the grand sweep of Elizabethan dance moves.
Be attracted
to every single thing, every single where.
Answer the future's italicized question
with a question.
Side swipe fundamental precepts
with a stolen car.
Curl up in a bell curve
carved on a cedar plank.
Dream you're ricocheting
in your sweet baby's powdered arms.
Follow your mother's advice
to an irreducible crisp.
Sleep on the burnt edge of a rye field.
Stuff sweet nothings
in the cosmos' shell-like ear.
And if and when
all is lost and found
unwrap the double-helix
with a wave of your sexy wax hand.

Oregon in March

Last night the earth
passed through the tail of a comet
and this morning the ornamental
plums are foolhardy
extroverts in sunshine
brazing their puffy genitalia.
It's spring again in the north.
Even the giant retarded oaks
try to sprout in this
sleek afterbirth of winter.
Seagulls pepper the ball fields.
Men from the retiree home worry about their hats.
Hello Sir, your green sweater is in bloom again.
Hello Ma'am, isn't walking grand?
Even the parked cars are free
to mount each other in public.
Mrs. Davis dons her kimono and walks for beer.
The Mitchells finally decide on blue for the living room.
How the metallic sun ruins our dulled perception.
Green flutters here
a strip of yellow flashes there.
March sneezes, mid-month
and birds fly
out of the arms of strangers.

Four Events in the Life of the Artist

Feeling floor tiles' canyon-like seams
through the soles of his shoes
the hall monitor nun
tries but fails
to introduce him to hell.

Watching wind and leaves' intimacy unfold
through the window over his boss's shoulder
glossy new verbs
full of venom and blood
slip by wasted.

Lost in an olive grove's dappled shade
on the face-up label in his shopping basket
a married couple blasphemes
over nothing in the checkout line.

Surfacing in a crosswalk
from a forty-year dream
a hundred ornate things
batter his eye
walk and don't walk flashing.

What If

It Starts by Seeing

rays emanate
from a woman running her mouth at a meeting.
She doesn't exist
anymore, now that her aura
is fused to air
and she's surfing her own
solar wind.

Fiddling with a pencil
she's about to become immaterial.

Yesterday, I walked through a field
I've walked many times before
at sunset.
But this time cloud light and wind
vortexed seaweed poplars
through a pinhole viewfinder
dropping me at the exact geographic center
of an irreducible flux.

And I just stood there.

It starts by seeing
everything drift
toward the same vanishing vanishing point.

It ends at a fire
watching wood be something else.

Bell Makers

Deep inside a remnant slice
of ancient forest
bird-like Shinto priests
chant ancient words
having sold everything else.

Stacked like wood at the end
of a footpath, they sleep for weeks
smudged by incense, dream-mumbling
until work wakes them
and the polestar guides them
along a path of venerated bone
to a hidden cave
where they take turns
pumping bellows and pouring iron.

And when the forging's cooled
and the meditation stops
they gather in a clearing
to swing a half-ton log
like a battering ram
into a one-ton bell
falling in and out of consciousness together
under the eaves of giant cedars.

Old as Dirt

Yes a crisis flutters
at the heart of a cobra lily
but it won't last long.

Nor the boy's pudgy hand
in his father's pudgy hand
in a park that won't be
a park much longer.

You and I already know
about a tuft of fur on birch bark
and the mile-wide river
nudging our caskets downstream.
We've already won
an all-inclusive, endless-night stay
in the undulating weave of our choice.

But my grandson, for Christ's sake.
Two years old. Old as dirt.
Even he knows.

Something whispered his name.
He heard it over the din.

A Man Walks

west across Kansas
with a suitcase in December.
Crows follow him.
Police discover
a contraband snowstorm
in his bag and run away.
He sleeps standing up
strapped to a power pole
dovetails sky to land
walks in a grain elevator's
thirty-mile shadow.
When he reaches the mountains
he turns around and begins again
each step finding
its former boot hole.
Blowing snow sculpts a bow shock
at the base of a fencepost.
Wind pins paper
against a tree.

Blackberry Preambles

•

Wanting to eat, we eat blackberries.
Wanting to make love, we eat blackberries.

•

A seed swells in the imprint
lovers leave in cemetery grass.

•

A man with purple fingers and shredded shirtsleeves
walks into a bar . . .

•

Mid-August. Daydreaming courthouse workers
roll downhill on their lunch break.

•

Open my fingers and look in my palm.
See how ripe the glossy is?

•

You know that abandoned railroad trestle off highway 47?
It too will be assimilated.

•

In the purple trunks, blackberries.
In the crimson trunks, the flesh and blood of Jesus Christ.

•

The Sun stores its excess in the thorns.
But not only in the thorns.

Reforming Science

What if the horizon really were the unlipped edge
of the good flat earth
and the ocean poured over it
into the deep unknown.

And what if no matter how well your lens was polished
the mountains of the moon
Jupiter's dance and Saturn's ears
were just your lashed-eye's irritant.

And what if a capitalized hoary verb
really did crest
the tower of babble, as the old book says
cleaving question from answer
seeding the periodic chart
and scattering the tribes.

Is there even a here and now?

The Whisper Came First

Desert Hike

Fine grit sand and my two hands
may be all it takes
to grow strawberries here.

Lizard tracks
zipping and unzipping the pleistocene
don't care what I do with this decade.

Not the mystery splashed across the great canvas arc.
Not this chaff blown in from the last millennium
pinwheeling its way to the next.

Just my two hands
sifting through what's left of the genesis jewel.

Sun inside wind.
Handwritten pages carried off by birds.

Oregon in Summer

Daybreak and gold's silver spectrum.

A muslin dress on a clothesline.

Dozing in an unoccupiable chemistry.

Birds everywhere and nowhere.

The background hiss in the palm of my hand.

for LB

It was your turn apparently.
Like you'd spent your quota
of hot showers, breathless views and gasoline.

Maybe you felt faint at first
getting up too fast
for a glass of water
and when the faint grew thicker
instead of fading away
maybe the transparency
suspended in blue
just gave way.

In my version, you had enough time
to tell yourself goodbye.

Perfume and car keys.
An impression on the sofa.
It's true what they say about April.
Overnight, heavy rain
washed the dust off everything.

Eternity's the Tree Branch

after a bird flies away

and the space the branch replaced.

It's a trail of pollen a mile long
carried by your whispered name

and a cricket's call asleep between heartbeats.

It's where dust blankets everything
and sunlight warms a lake.

Run your fingers through waist-high grass.
Run your fingers through waist-high grass.

Whispers

•

Dry for days
shirts on a clothesline
anchor the afternoon.
An open window lets the premonition in.
Someone he knew passed in the night.

•

A year-long digression
inside a private conversation with himself
finally winds down.
The void fills with water. Insect hum.
A dozen stars link arms
so not to fly apart.

•

A metropolis polluted by teamwork
conspires to consume
more plastic.
Atop the newest monolith
the boy mayor flips a switch
killing the last memory
of illuminated monks.

•

From the lotus position
at the bottom of a swimming pool
the manufactured memory of a bird
in his outstretched palm
rises to the surface and flies away.

•

A cicada's call
stopped a man's heart here once.
In this very place
running water carried fallen leaves away.

born naked

a heartbeat thaws you
from absolute silence
and dumps you into time
where your nerves conspire with wolves
to howl at the polar moon
and live forever
but of course you can't
do that and at the end
of time you slip
under the same icy swells you surfaced in
to rejoin the roar
you once called silence
finding what you never lost
the aurora the howling
was all about

Divinity's In

whatever envelope
eternity's in.

Tadpoles suspended in reed water.
Gnats backlit in a shaft of sunlight.

In you too, a slice luminescent enough
to build a church around.

Hurtling toward Andromeda's embrace
everywhere grassland
is about to go to seed.

In the Age of Rocks

when shorelines inched upslope at night
and the north star sang
old songs about the big bang
and all the world's rubble
was sequestered in the ice sheets

a drifting voice lifted
off the surface of a lake
found a man to inhale it
and pass it to others
and them to others still
until they all succumbed.

Everywhere the earth hadn't felt
their footsteps yet
the whisper came first.

Muted birds, far off.
Soil red before the drumbeat fell.

Very Little Needs

Some Things

are as simple as a gate
half open in a downpour.

Everyone dodges something.
Bullets or words
gooseflesh at the sight
of our own child's oracle eyes.
Explaining is a pillow for the living.

Today it's a cemetery's ornamental arched bridge
and the creek below it
I'm trying to ignore
visiting my father's grave.

Very little needs
to be said: He's lucky
to own some small wedge of rich black earth.
A little rain.
Pine needles.

So Well

I sit in what passes for a plaza
analyzing everything
waiting for a sunburn that won't come.

A genius silently gesticulates
Mozart in the square.
He knows only one dance
but knows it so well.
I drop a coin in his overturned hat.
A scrap of paper flutters.

Somewhere basalt
greets another wave.
A train recycles
the route of its derailment
while a woman in the dining car
traces the outline
of an unsuitable suitor
in the palm of her transparent hand.

I make a list
of verbs that mean sleep
and then sleep.

Here's what I know:
Two seconds of geologic time.
The difference between a sigh.

Yard Work

It's good to be back
in love again
with the unnamed weeds
and their companions
the other unnamed weeds.
Green in a sea of green.

I could, like my neighbors
poison them if I wanted
a crime pre-alibied by advertising.
But I see myself
in the tall, single stemmed ones
a red streak in each green leaf
crowned when spent
with an isolate white bloom
an exclamation mark at the end
of a four-billion-year-old sentence.

It took forever this time
for embers to warm enough
to pull me over the chasm
back into life.
But they did, and now I'm in dirt
with weeds again
sleepy in sunshine
lucky beyond words.

Having Nothing to Say

isn't such a bad thing
after all, what can be built with words
but a trim, pollinated affluence
diluted on a breeze.

Here I am again. Paper, pencil
waiting at an open window.
Moss grows on one side of an oak.
It drops a piece of branch.

I live in a very small town.
An older gentleman
silent long before his wife died
walks home from the convenience store
with a few necessities.

Rain stops.
He steps from lotus to lotus.

Anatomy

When someone lifts a hand
to your mouth, you should know
what's in it, a heart
shaped stone or a tiny umbrella
turned upside down
a birdbath full of flowers.

In Holland people wear wooden shoes
and they know when they're being followed.
They know how to read
the map of the palm, how to plan
hunger around moments of clarity.
They know if, in a hand
there is something edible.

Dear Person, take this string
and swallow it.
This hand is a cloud of emotion
an anchor of the heart.
It sinks into something aqua.
It tears into something tender.

This Poem Exists

because long ago we sat under a tree
and reshaped it into a fountain
with perfectly oxygenated words.

And because that tree became a cocoon
when an unexpected kiss passed between us
erasing everything we said
before and after.

Now, thirty years later, I'm wondering
if anything can shore up
this sand pile beneath me
the wind and rain I have
being no good at that kind of work.

Some days the sun still shines
directly on me and I strut
across whatever part of this naked earth I'm on
reborn.

Other days I drift
in dust kicked up
over an empty ball field
by wind and whatever
bastard memory comes along.

Repeating the Thank You

I jump up
then down.
Now I'm breathing under water.
That's how it works.
I can't put you back.

You're eating soup
at the edge of the world
peering over the top
of a book you're holding upside down.

Let's say I actually could
unwind your clock for a second.
Maybe our shared veneer
would turn out to be an infinity loop?

This warm pile of maple leaves and I
chase you across the earth's terminator
to say thank you
for wood smoke
Michigan hardwoods
footfalls in moccasins
soup.

Exercise

I walk around the block
pretending to care a scrap about my health
remembering a distant youth
as if it belonged to me.

These days there's little left
to keep me upright
but my own skin
catching a stiff wind at the corner.
But once I actually was
barefoot, submerged in kisses even
dozing off with what's-her-name Cavanaugh
on damp grass under a hardwood.

We all spin in the same eddy
trying to spot the same north star.
We all meet for coffee
trying to defibrillate
an old friend's stained-glass heart.
How much can be said
exactly equals
how far apart
whatever and etcetera are.

I'm walking among shops now
a compliant, negligent force
weaving in and out of foot traffic.

Soon I'll drift into the local bakery
find a gem in the day-old bin
and pass it by.

Self-Portrait

A fractal rendition of a bamboo grove.

Defending an ancient virus over a glass of red wine.

Hand-feeding a nascent awareness sequestered on a lily pad.

Piercing a distant epoch with a #2 pencil.

Lost in the ancient wilds between strawberry seeds.

Trying to fertilize everything.

About the Author

JOHN HARN

was born in Dayton, Ohio, grew up near Detroit and attended Michigan State University. After graduating with a BA in Education, he spent a year in Galveston, Texas, working at the Community Arts Center on the Strand. In 1978, he joined the MFA Poetry program at the University of Oregon in Eugene where he was an advisee of Ralph Salisbury. He taught introductory poetry writing there for two years and for one year at the Oregon State Penitentiary in Salem. His first daughter Emily was born to Jane Clugston in Eugene in 1980. In the mid-eighties, he taught ESL in Nagoya, Japan and after that, at Pacific University in Forest Grove, Oregon. He married Etsuko Matsunaga in Japan in 1989 and they opened an ESL school in Portland, which they operated for 16 years. Daughter Jessica was born in 1991, followed by Michelle in 1994. In 2010, he self-published a 500-page book on his family's genealogy and history, available for free at *harn-ancestry.com*. His first grandchild, Abraham, was born in 2014. He currently lives, writes, tries to live off coffee and takes long walks for inspiration in Nashville.

Acknowledgements

Anima (UK)
    Desert Hike
    This Ecstasy Because
California Quarterly
    Everything You Took
    So Well
    Reforming Science
Carolina Quarterly
    Walk Forever
Chariton Review
    Blackberry Preambles
Cloudbank
    Exercise
    Passport
Cutbank
    Anatomy
Denver Quarterly
    Self Portrait
Hotel Amerika
    Daily Walk
Innisfree Poetry Journal
    Maybe It Should Go Unnoticed
    Having Nothing to Say
Pinyon Review
    Old as Dirt
Pleiades
    Because the Economic Imperative
Post Road Magazine
    Yard Work
    Jewelry On
Red Rock Review
    This Poem Exists
South Carolina Review
    It Starts by Seeing

CPSIA information can be obtained
at www.ICGtesting.com
Printed in the USA
FSOW01n2051210917
39059FS